Railways in Northamptc ~~~~~~

and the Soke of Pe

on old picture po

Andrew Swift

1. A single-coach train at **Woodford Halse** on the Great Central Railway. This ran to Byfield, two miles away, to connect with Blisworth-Stratford upon Avon trains. In the early years of the Great Central, there was a through coach from Marylebone to Stratford. This was attached to the rear of the 6.20pm Sheffield express and uncoupled at speed south of Woodford. It drifted into the station under its own momentum before being coupled to another engine and taken to Stratford. This card was issued by the Locomotive Publishing Company in the 1920's.

2. Finedon Station signalbox. Finedon station on the Midland Main Line was almost two miles from the town. At one time there were ironworks near the station, but by the time it closed in December 1940 these had long gone.

INTRODUCTION

Since my first book on Northamptonshire Railway Stations - on which I collaborated with Alan Rice - came out earlier this year, many new cards have turned up. As a second printing of that book is now being issued, it seems an appropriate time to present some of this new material in a second volume. This time I have not confined myself to views of stations but included other aspects of the railway scene - sheds, viaducts, horse-drawn wagons, and - most important - the people who worked and travelled on the railway.

The cards I have included are a mixture of "commercial" cards which were sold at normal retail outlets, including station bookstalls, and "private" cards issued by the photographers themselves. These had a much more limited circulation. But all give a fascinating glimpse into a part of Northamptonshire's past which has long gone.

In the introduction to the last book, I stated that Northamptonshire once had *"around 90 stations"* - this led to correspondence in the local press as to the exact number. Inside the back cover of this book I have included a list of stations in the old county with opening and closing dates. I don't expect that my list will put an end to the debate, but I hope it will be useful contribution to it.

Andrew Swift
Findedon, November 1999

3. *"I am sending you a card for your album of Harringworth Viaduct with the River Welland in flood,"* runs the message on this card sent from Northampton to Great Yarmouth on 25th July 1909. The viaduct, six miles north of Corby, was built by the Midland Railway in 1876-78. Three-quarters of a mile long and with 82 arches, it is still used by freight and occasional passenger trains.

4. Another flood at **Braunston & Willoughby** station (north-west of Daventry) caused by the sudden melting of a late fall of snow. A policeman watches as a traction engine (out of view to the right) hauls an early motor vehicle to dry land. The weight of the snow has also brought the telegraph wires down. But the Great Central Railway, riding high above the battered landscape, carried on regardless.

5. A card published by Les Hanson which captures the 1930's railway scene. On 1st June 1936 a southbound train heads out of **Northampton Castle** station, passing the Peterborough bay platforms - now just a memory - on the left.

NORTHAMPTON

10786

6. Also no more than a memory is **Northampton shed,** seen here on a Locomotive Publishing Company card from the 1920's. The shed was alongside the Grand Union Canal in Far Cotton and closed in 1965.

7. How many people parking in St John's Car Park in Northampton realise that there was once a station here, carried on arches high above the road? **Northampton St John's** opened in 1872 and was the Midland Railway's second station in the town. The first, which lasted from 1866 to 1872, faced the **LNWR** station on Bridge Street. Trains ran from St John's to Kettering and Bedford. The station closed to passengers in 1939, and services were diverted to Northampton Castle.

8. Northampton's first station opened at Far Cotton (known locally as Frog Island) in 1845. In the 1860's, Bradshaw's (publishers of the national railway timetable) referred to it as "Cotten End," but in 1876 the railway company decided to call it **Bridge Street**, the name it kept until closure in 1964. Although a single track still runs through the station site, no trace of the station remains.

9. The only postcard view of **Castle Ashby & Earl's Barton** station known to exist. It is unusual, in that it was taken from a carriage window. The unknown photographer obviously didn't consider it worth getting off the train! The "Station Hotel" (in the background) was the only building at this spot apart from the station. It is now a private house. After closure, the station was demolished, but the goods shed on the far side of the level crossing has been converted into Dunkley's restaurant.

10. Look up **Ditchford** on the map, and all you'll find is a bridge a couple of miles east of Wellingborough. Why somebody should want to build a station there is a mystery. But they did, and for almost 80 years the trains continued to call. On this card from around 1905 the entire population of Ditchford - stationmaster John Lymage and his family - stands on the down platform as a photographer records this curious backwater for posterity.

IRTHLINGBOROUGH STATION.

11 & 12. Irthlingborough station was so far away from Irthlingborough that it was originally known as Higham Ferrers. It was near the medieval bridge over the Nene. A little community grew up around the station, including two pubs - the "Railway Inn" and the "Fitzwilliam Arms." It closed in 1964 and all trace of it has disappeared. A conveyor belt for gravel has been built on the trackbed, the traffic roars past on the flyover above, and this is all.

NENE OVER FALL RINGSTEAD

13. Think of a summer's afternoon. Of a leisurely journey down the Nene. A window seat in an empty compartment. Wood panelling. Deep cushions thick with dust. Smoke drifting in through the open window. Dragonflies dipping past on bright wings. High clouds. The smell of new mown grass. A sudden roar of water tipping over sluices. The train hammering across a little bridge. A mill wheel turning. That was **Ringstead**. This card was sent from Thrapston to Stoke on Trent on 12th August 1914: *"My dear Gran, Connie and I have been here nearly a fortnight and are going home tomorrow. We have had a lovely time and feel much better for the change. We have spent all our time in the fields and have had lovely weather. Meg."* Meg fails to mention that war had broken out a week earlier. It mustn't have seemed that important.

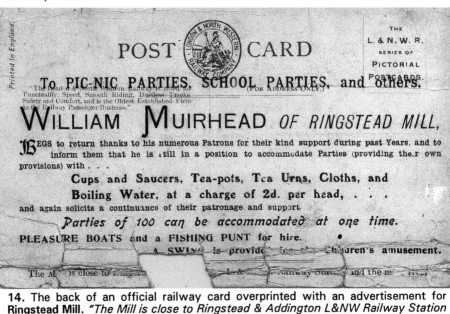

14. The back of an official railway card overprinted with an advertisement for **Ringstead Mill**. *"The Mill is close to Ringstead & Addington L&NW Railway Station and the main river"* runs the message - partly obliterated - at the bottom of the card.

15. Ringstead & Addington station was some distance from the villages it was supposed to serve. Nevertheless it survived until closure of the Nene Valley line in 1964. This early card of the station conveys a sense of the loneliness which staff at this isolated spot must have felt on a misty winter's morning. But in the summer, with the Nene flowing virtually past their door, it would have been a different story. The stationmaster on this early card is Frederick George, later stationmaster at Irthlingborough.

16. Wigsthorpe Crossing was between Thorpe and Barnwell, where the railway crossed a minor road east of the road from Thrapston to Oundle. Unfortunately there is no information on the back of the card and the identity of these two women posing in front of the little crossing keeper's hut sometime around 1910 must remain a mystery - unless somebody knows different.

17. Although the village of **Elton** (north of Oundle) was in Huntingdonshire, the station which bore its name was in Northamptonshire. A striking feature of the station was the massive chimney stack on the stationmaster's house. In the late nineteenth century, the London & North Western Railway opened large ballast quarries near the station. The ballast was loaded into wagons in Elton yard for use all over the company's system. Elton station closed to both goods and passengers in 1953.

18. Next station up the line was **Wansford** - and although the station was in Huntingdonshire, the village two miles away from which it took its name was in Northamptonshire. Today, both station and village are in Cambridgeshire. In this view from around 1937, an experimental railcar stands at the end of the platform. Two of these petrol-driven vehicles were built at Coventry, but, despite extensive trials, were not taken into stock. Wansford station closed in 1957, but reopened twenty years later as the headquarters of the preserved Nene Valley Railway.

19. **Castor** station, five miles west of Peterborough, opened in 1847, two years after the Nene Valley line was built. Its meagre facilities stand in stark contrast to the magnificent buildings elsewhere on the line. It attracted little traffic, and in later years few trains called. Probably the most exciting thing ever to happen at Castor was when a German VI rocket exploded nearby in January 1945.

20. The stone-built station at **Barnack** on the Stamford-Wansford branch. An early card published by A Webster of Barnack. The branch was built by the Marquis of Burghley in 1867. It closed to passengers in 1929.

21. Helpston station, dating from 1846, was six miles north of Peterborough on the Midland Railway's line to Stamford and Leicester. Helpston's main claim to fame is as the birthplace of the "peasant poet," John Clare, who died in Northampton Asylum in 1864. Helpston station closed in 1966, but the level crossing, which straddles both the Peterborough-Leicester line and the main line from London to York, is still very much in use.

22. Even in the golden age of railways the Great Northern station at **Peterborough** had a decidedly dusty look to it, although the wonderful collection of enamel signs on the fence went some way towards brightening it up. The station opened in 1850 and had several changes of name - Peterborough Priestgate, Peterborough Cowgate, Peterborough North, and finally - after Peterborough East station closed in 1966 - plain Peterborough. It was completely rebuilt in the 1970's.

New Bridge over G.N.R. Peterboro.

23. The Crescent Bridge at **Peterborough** was opened in April 1913 at a cost of £34,000 - around £1.5m in today's money. Up till then, there were two sets of level crossings with a short gap between them. It can't have been much fun for drivers of horse-drawn vehicles to be stuck between two sets of locked gates with engines whistling fore and aft. The large number of postcards featuring the bridge testify to the pride - and the relief - the people of Peterborough must have felt when it was eventually built.

24. *"Dear Winnie - this was taken in the other week. Can you recognise me? Hope you are all well. With love, Malcolm."* So runs the message on this card sent from Peterborough to Cambridge at 11.45pm on 23rd February 1906. They're all wearing Great Eastern Railway cap or lapel badges, so this is likely to be the Great Eastern Station at **Peterborough,** which opened in 1845 and closed in 1966. But which one's Malcolm?

25. A London-bound express thunders out of **Peterborough** just before the First World War - a picture that sums up the grime and glory of the golden age of steam.

26. Not hard to see why young train spotters saved up for a day trip to **Peterborough** in the days of steam. A streamlined A4 loco - stablemate of *Mallard* which notched up the steam world record of 126 mph a few miles north of Peterborough on 3rd July 1938 - stands in the station with a northbound express. For the record, this is No. 4900 *Gannet.* All around is evidence of the goods traffic which was once the lifeblood of the railways, while in the background, the Early English cathedral dominates the scene.

27. Salvage workers hold pieces of Edwardian china, undamaged amid the devastation caused by this Midland Railway smash at **Peterborough's** Crescent Bridge in 1922.

28. *"I am sending you a p/c of Boughton Crossing - this is Jenny Cave standing by the gate,"* runs the message on this card posted from Northampton in August 1908. Today, the location is familiar to walkers and cyclists as the southern end of the Brampton Valley Way, which follows the trackbed of the old line from Northampton to Market Harborough.

29. This card of **Pitsford and Brampton** by an unknown publisher evokes the magic of the country station in the years before the First World War. A two-coach local train runs in from the north past a workman leaning on his shovel, while a porter stands ready with the mails. One of the boy porters turns to glance at the camera. A lady in her Edwardian finery waits with her companion as the train draws in. Four staff, two passengers - it was a common enough ratio for the country station. Today, Pitsford is the headquarters of the Northampton & Lamport Railway.

30. A domestic idyll at the little wayside station of **Harringworth**, north of Corby, in 1912. The man on the left is probably William Gale, who was stationmaster at Harringworth in 1914. The station served a village of around 250 people and closed in 1948, the year the railways were nationalised.

31. Lady porters at the Midland Railway station in Wellingborough during the First World War.

32. A local train calls at **Harringworth** station in the late twenties or early thirties. The real interest here, though, is the box. Built in 1928, it survived until 1998, when Balfour Beatty won a contract to resignal and upgrade the Kettering-Manton line. The box was surplus to requirements, and they offered it to the Northampton & Lamport Railway, based at Pitsford, who took it away on Sunday 7th June 1998.

33. Superb - the only word to describe this card, dating from 1909, of the G
platform, the improvised bookstall - and those signs and posters: *"HASTIN*
& BOULOGNE" - *"CHEAP HOLIDAY TOURS TO HULL"* (Hull!?) - *"FRY'S C*
empty platform. They had reason to be cheerful. The station was just ten
the tracks would be ripped up and the station turned into a tyre and exha

...d station at **Brackley**. Just look at that ornate "Try Your Weight" machine, the spotless
..T LEONARDS" - "RAMSGATE" - "STEAMSHIP TICKETS: BEST BERTHS" - "CALAIS
..E" - "SCHWEPPES" - "GENTLEMEN." The four staff stand grinning on an otherwise
..nd was built to last for ever. How were they to know that, less than a century later,

34. Although only seven miles from the large loco sheds at Wellingborough, **Kettering** had a shed of its own. Here a line-up of vintage locos is seen in the yard. On this card, from a photograph taken by H.C. Casserley on 3rd September 1933, the houses in Station Road can be seen in the background. The occasion was probably an enthusiasts' outing - witness the three young men jotting down numbers on the right. Kettering shed closed in 1965 and was demolished to make way for a car park.

35. On a card published by Spencer Percival a cyclist, decked out in all the latest gear, stands on **Kettering** station. He could almost have stepped out of the pages of *Three Men in a Boat*. At the time most of the cards in this book were published, cycling was the only real alternative to horses or shanks's pony. And for longer journeys, the train held undisputed monopoly.

36. A view of **Corby Ironworks** on a card sent from Gretton to a Miss Quinney at Hinwick House, near Wellingborough, on 13th May 1911. *"Gretton lost at cricket here today. This is a snap of Corby Furnises (sic) with my Kodak. I hope to send you some PCs I take now and again... Yours ever, John."* The Ironworks opened in 1910 and in 1911, the year this photo was taken, there was a prolonged and bitter strike for union recognition.

37. Corby steelworks, built in the early 1930's, tower above a diminutive tank engine. The railways feeding iron ore to the furnaces at Corby were part of a network of lines which once covered vast tracts of the county. Now the only reminders of them are the nature reserves and country parks which have sprung up along the abandoned tracks.

38. Staff pose outside the Midland Railway's station at **Desborough and Rothwell**. A fine example of the sort of architecture which proclaimed the railway's pride, and its confidence in the future. Although the station closed to passengers in 1968, this building is still standing and is now a private house.

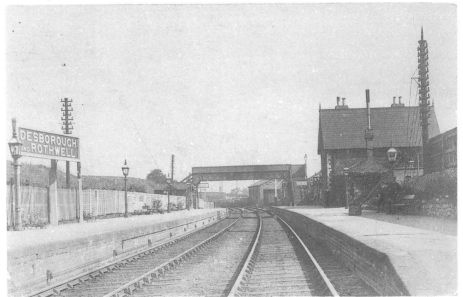

39. Another view of **Desborough and Rothwell** on a card sent from Kettering to Leicester around 1910. *"The newsboy on the platform is Harry, he is now working for Smith & Sons at Desboro'."*

40. A Midland Railway horse and cart stand outside **Irchester** station on a card sent from Wellingborough to Bedford in 1905. The poster on the wall advertises the opening of Heysham Harbour and the introduction of new sailings to Ireland on 1st September 1904. Irchester station, near Knuston Hall, closed in 1960.

41. An "express" parcels wagon stands outside the Midland station at **Wellingborough.** The steps in the background have long since disappeared.

42. Steam drifts from the engine of the Higham branch train as it stands at **Wellingborough** on a dull, miserable day. The Higham branch closed to regular passenger trains in 1959 and this part of Wellingborough station has since been demolished.

43. A view inside the roundhouse at **Wellingborough** in June 1936. A record from 1920 shows that 91 locos were allocated to Wellingborough. In the Second World War the RAF staged dummy bombing raids on Wellingborough yard to assess the impact of chemical bombardment - an indication of its strategic importance. The last steam engine was withdrawn from Wellingborough on 13th June 1964 and the roundhouse, dating from 1868, was demolished a month later.

44 & 45. Two cards showing the railway scene around **Wellingborough** in the early 1930's from the camera of Les Hanson. In the first a Midland Railway three-cylinder compound heads south past the old Irthlingborough Ironworks - now the Laurence Leyland Industrial Complex - on 9th June 1930.

The second view gives some idea of just how busy Wellingborough was in the days of steam. In the background, half obscured by smoke, is the railwaymen's hostel on Finedon Road, now no more than a fading memory.

46. A distant view of **Wellingborough London Road** station on the Nene Valley line. It closed to passengers in 1964 and today the site of the station is dominated by the A45 flyover. This card by an unknown publisher was sent from Bedford in 1906.

47. The driver of a tank engine takes time off from shunting to stare at the camera, while **Higham Ferrers** church dominates the background. The Rushden Historical Transport Society are currently relaying the track between Rushden and Higham. Who knows - one day a "past and present" photo could be taken from the same spot. For the record, the loco in the picture is Johnson 0-4-4T 1P Class No. 1230.

48. On 9th March 1899, the directors of the newly completed Great Central Railway made a trip from Sheffield to London Marylebone. The parish councillors of **Woodford Halse** assumed the train would stop at their station, and drew up an address to deliver to the directors. Dressed in all their pomp and finery, they waited on the platform for the train to arrive. Unfortunately, it passed through without stopping and the address had to be sent on by post. This view of Woodford station dates from around 1910.

49. On this card of **Woodford** station, sent from Rugby station on 31st August 1906, Fred Cox, Bill Woods, Fred Holmes, Jim Coulson (recorded as stationmaster in 1914) and (?) Chambers line up for the camera. Among the destinations listed on the name board are Portsmouth, Cheltenham, Bath, Cardiff, Plymouth and Dover.

50. An evocative shot of an up express just south of **Charwelton** station at 2.39pm on Saturday 3rd July 1937. The locomotive is LNER No. 5505 *Ypres*, and the card was produced by Les Hanson, who has been recording the railway scene in Northamptonshire and beyond for well over 60 years. Standing in this same spot today, it is almost impossible to tell that there was once a main line here.

51. Brackley Viaduct, about 400 yards south of Brackley station and 756 feet long, was built of blue brick and originally had 23 arches. Due to land movement, the last two arches on the south side were replaced by iron plate spans. This card, published by Valentine of Dundee, was sent from Brackley to Barnsley on 16th September 1913. The viaduct was demolished after the closure of the Great Central Railway.

52. In the days of steam, water troughs were provided on main lines so that locomotives could refill their tanks without stopping. These are the troughs at **Charwelton** on the Great Central Railway. They were 874 yards long. Water was pumped from Hollerwell Pool by the pump house, which can be seen in the background. This photograph was taken by H. Gordon Tidey and published as a postcard by the Locomotive Publishing Company in the 1920's.

WOODFORD RUNNING SHEDS, GREAT CENTRAL RAILWAY.

By The Locomotive Publishing Company Ltd., London.

53. An early card by the Locomotive Publishing Co, showing **Woodford shed.** which held up to £110000. The shed and sidings were built on a 06 acre site, most of it on an embankment built from spoil from nearby Catesby Tunnel. In 1914, over 300 men worked on the railway at Woodford.

54. Two porters assume a nonchalant pose for the camera at **Kilsby & Crick** station, between Rugby and Long Buckby.

55. A superb panoramic view of a Weedon to Leamington train approaching **Braunston** station. Hedgerows thick with blossom, meadows thick with trees: the English pastoral landscape before the First World War. This little line never saw much traffic. The Weedon-Daventry branch opened in 1888 and was extended to Leamington in 1895. It closed just over 60 years later in 1958.

56 & 57. On 14th August 1915, near **Weedon** on the West Coast Main Line, a coupling rod on a locomotive travelling on the down line worked loose and smashed into the sleepers on the up line. This pushed the track out of alignment just as the Irish Mail was approaching. The horrific results can be seen on these two cards, nos. 1 and 3 in a series by an unknown publisher. 10 people were killed and 64 injured. Just over 36 years later, on 21st September 1951, Weedon was the scene of another accident, when a Liverpool-Euston express left the rails and plunged down the embankment. On that occasion 15 people died and 36 were injured.

58. In this view of **Blisworth,** the West Coast Main Line sweeps majestically past in the background, while in the foreground a scattering of makeshift chicken coops keeps watch over the single line to Stratford as it ambles off into the wilds of Northamptonshire. The single-road engine shed on the left was deemed surplus to requirements in 1929 and went to Towcester to become a warehouse. However, this card was not sent through the post until 1934.

59. And here we are again. The date is 3rd April 1937 and the sun is shining. The shed has gone, but the turntable is still in use. But forget about them, and look at this magnificent Stanier loco at the head of a down express, milk tanks marshalled between the carriages: the West Coast Main Line at its most magnificent.

60. The world we have lost. A miniature railway connected **Blakesley Hall,** near Towcester, with Blakesley Station, three-quarters of a mile away. It carried coal and supplies to the hall as well as occasional visitors. No trace remains. The hall, the station and the miniature railway have all been swept away. The photographer, F.C. Coleman of Darlington, records on the back that the loco was built by Bassett-Lowke of Northampton.

61. Off to Blisworth for a spot of spotting. In 1938, a young man stands at the door of the first compartment as his brother - I Hs Hanson - takes a picture of the battered Victorian tank engine which will take them from **Northampton Castle** to Blisworth for an afternoon by the West Coast Main Line.

ELD STATION.

C904

62. **Byfield,** on the single track line from Blisworth to Stratford-up-Avon, is typical of the scores of country stations which once graced the Northamptonshire countryside. Some time around 1910, the crew of a goods train line up beside three local smokers for a passing photographer. Byfield closed almost half a century ago - in 1952. Go there today and you'd never know a railway existed. How can something so substantial, which had such an impact on people's lives, have disappeared so completely, leaving hardly even a memory behind?

63. There were once plans to build a large steelworks at **Irthlingborough.** The Ebbw Vale Steel, Iron & Coal Company started to dig mines there during the First World War, and in 1917 the Sinter Ore Crushing Plant, featured on this card, was built by Hanson & Sons of Wellingborough. *"This is a snap shot taken on the works of our loco,"* runs the message on this card sent from Irthlingborough to Southampton in 1917. *"I am on the picture but will leave it to you to discover my whereabouts. Best wishes and love from Cecil."* The steelworks were never built but ore from the mines was shipped to Ebbw Vale for processing until 1965.

64. You could do a "past & present" version of this shot. You could - but you'd have to stand on the down track of the West Coast Main Line to do it. This is the "Anchor Inn" by **Banbury Lane Crossing** at Gayton near Blisworth. Directly behind the pub was the Grand Union Canal and Gayton Wharf. Today the "Anchor" is a private house and the wharf is closed, but the canal and railway are still very much in business. A bridge is to be built here to replace the level crossing.